🌹 A WORLD OF LOVE AND MYSTERY

A
WORLD
OF
LOVE
AND
MYSTERY

WALDEN SCOTT CRAM

REPRINTED IN PAPERBACK 2015
AT THE UNIVERSITY OF TORONTO PRESS

To
the Memory
of
My Wife
Olive N. Cram

Foreword

To the loveliness I see and hear in field and river,
mountain, lake, and sky;
To the world of fancy, wonder, mystery I dimly feel
but cannot fully grasp and make my own;
To the touch of friendly hands, the thrill of
understanding hearts, the kindly look and sweet communion
with those I know, and those I call my own;
To the memories of the yesteryears that bring to me the
loves, the joys, the sorrows, and the triumphs of
the days;
To the thoughts of men inscribed on printed page, thoughts
sublime of seer, of poet, of prophet, and of saint;
To these I pay my humble tribute, for they are Windows
to the World through which there shines upon my life
a light, that tints and colours lonely hours with joy
and peace.

W. S. C.

Contents

PART ONE

I Wonder How They All Can Be
And What They Mean to You and Me

> I have felt
> A presence that disturbs me with the joy
> Of elevated thoughts.
>
> WORDSWORTH, Tintern Abbey.

So Many Are the Things I Like

So many are the things I like
On earth, in ocean, air, and sky.

I like the stars that shine on high.
I like the tiny, tiny buds
That promise leaves, and flowers, and fruit;
The humming bird, so richly dressed,
That seems to stand in very air
To suck the honey from the flower.

I like to sit beside a pool
To watch the birds that come and go,
To see them drink, and dip their wings,
And spray their heads and bodies o'er.

I like the pansies, modest, lowly,
That look like human faces, small,
Gazing upwards with a smile,
And greeting me as I stand near.

I like the waving fields of grain;
The tall and spreading stalks of corn;
The red tomatoes on the vines;
The big ripe pumpkins on the ground.

I like the shimmer of the moon
Upon the ripples of the lake,
And the great bow across the sky,
The rainbow arch with wealth of colour.

So many, many things I like.
There's so much charm and loveliness,
Sometimes I sit, and sit, and think,
And wonder how they all can be,
And what they mean to you and me.

Each Flower a Thought

We are twelve rose buds in this quaint old vase,
We have brought you greetings from the far away,
We share with you all the joys that are ours,
We wish you all that flowers can say.

I smile upon these red rose buds
In the quaint old vase upon my stand.
They charm me with their loveliness
As they breathe on me the love of friends.
For flowers are pages that I read
In God's Great Book of Living Things—
Each flower a thought, a silent thought,
Of friendship, beauty, hope, and cheer.

Companions in My Little World

I look about me in my suite
At chairs and tables, couch and bed,
At lamps, and stove, and plants, and books,
At dresser, pictures, dishes, clothes,
At all the little things I have.

Some yield rich gifts of memories sweet.
Some reach far out to worlds of thought.
Some give me warmth and serve me well
In body's needs for life and strength.
But these, my plants, alone are living,
Alone share life with my own self.
And some there are of learnèd men,
Who think that shrubs, and trees, and plants
Can feel a something of the thrill,
The quiet thrill and joy of life.

I wonder do my plants e'er feel
What joy they give to me, alone—
Companions in my little world.

One Autumn Day

One autumn day I started out alone
Through woods that border on a lovely lake.
The path I travelled grew more faint, and fainter still.
I changed my course.
Soon, before me rose a fairy-land of colour,
Lovelier than aught I could in mind recall,
A grove of maples, all in autumn garb,
In tints of yellow, orange, and red—
Nature's free gift to all who walk her ways,
Who feel within their souls the peace and joy
Of her creative loveliness and life.

'Tis Winter in Our Northern Clime

The tiny flakes of falling snow,
They rest upon the hard, cold ground.
The trodden paths, the hills, the fields
Are covered o'er. The evergreens
Stand robed in white like magic witches.
'Tis winter in our northern clime.
Far as the human eye can see,
The charm of pure white crystal snow.
Yet in their beds down neath the snow
Sleep countless little seeds of trees,
Of plants, and grasses, grains, and shrubs.
They are not dead, they only sleep.

The Pride of the Prairies

Through the long winter months I rest in my earth bed,
Just alone by myself with the snow blanket o'er me.
I love Mother Earth, she seems part of my being,
For summer and winter she nestles about me.
I am hers, she is mine, we belong to each other.
The Spirit of Life, that is ever creating,
Has made me, has reared me from a seedling, so tiny,
A tiny, wee image of all that I shall be—
A purple spring crocus, the pride of the prairies.

With the first breath of spring I feel a motion, a tremor.
It's the quiet urge within from the Life-Stream Eternal,
That's pressing me upwards to fill my life mission.
There's a drawing, a beckoning from the sunlight above me
From the wide, open prairies that long for my presence.
We're friends through the years, I add charm to their vastnes,
Breathing joy midst the free, boundless spaces about me.
I feel I'm no stranger in this land of my kindred—
A purple spring crocus, the pride of the prairies.

Here in My Home in Canyon Deep

The years roll on. I feel the thrill,
The power of life within my roots,
As they spread inwards, make their way
Between rock layers in the cliff.
My branches reach out to the air,
My leaves are lifted towards the sun,
Far up above the whirling stream,
Above the depths of wave and tide
That day and night speed on and on,
And ever slowly, slowly cut
A deeper course through mountain rock.

So now I've grown to middle age,
A large fir tree, quite firmly set
Within the crevices of rock.
I've struggled hard to make a home.
I've lacked the shelter of my kind.
I've been so much just on my own.

But this I feel, as I look back,
The very struggle, winds, and storms
Have added firmness to my life.
I gladly welcome each new day.
Somehow within each leaf and branch
There flows new strength from sun and air,
Fresh strength to meet what each day brings,
Here in my home in canyon deep.

It's Such a Joy to Be a Robin

To-day I'm so happy, I've returned to the prairies.
A Something in Nature seems to beckon and guide us,
For here I was born, near here where I'm living,
On these wide, open prairies, so lovely in spring-time.

My bright red coat gives class and distinction.
I sing with the first streak of light on the skyline.
I sing to my mate from the trees in the garden.
I sing to the world as my heart fills with gladness.
. . . .

But now I must hasten to finish my story—
My mate at home is waiting, waiting.
I love my mate, she loves me too.
For years we've lived and worked together.
We've brought up broods, and sent them forth
As good Canadian prairie robins.
For years we think you've liked us too.
It's such a joy to be a robin.

That Little Knot Hole in Our Barn

A little knot hole in a barn,
'Twas entrance, exit for the birds,
The swallows that each year brought joy
To me in boyhood days. They wintered
Far away, but ne'er forgot
With each returning day of spring
The little knot hole in our barn.
In sheltered nooks within that barn
They built their nests and reared their young.

To-day across so many years,
And distant far from boyhood home,
I sit and muse. In fancy still
I see the swallows come and go.
I marvel at the care of Him,
Who taught them with unerring faith
To know their way, and find each spring
That little knot hole in our barn.

A Something Calls

One day there came a strange, new urge,
A Something that kept calling, calling,
And telling us that life's big venture
Now was dawning, coursing through us,
Beckoning us like chart and compass
Down the Thompson, through the Fraser,
Out into the great broad waters,
The salty waters of the ocean,
Where we lived for two years longer.

Then once more a Something called us.
We seemed to see the shallow waters
Beckoning us back home again.
We made our journey from the ocean,
Up the river, through the gorges,
Leaping high above the rapids,
On through waters, calmer, slower,
Round the bend into this brooklet,
Four long years since we were born here.

. . . .

But we must not linger longer.
A Something calls. We feel the mission
Of our life where we began it.

A few brief hours complete the cycle,
As we search out in the sand bars
Little hollows for our nesting,
Trusting to the perfect life plan,
Knowing that the Power that called us
Will lead our offspring on their mission.

And now our final journey's o'er.
We float quietly from the shallows.

'Tis the strange, mysterious story,
Nature's saga of the salmon.

Dreamland Pond

Tommy Runyon loved the beavers,
And in his sleep he thought he was one.
To him it seemed so wonderful
To live with them in Dreamland Pond.

Sometimes he swam, and dived, and played
At hide-and-seek amongst the lodges.
Sometimes he sported with the kittens,
The round and fluffy beaver kittens.

Tommy Runyon learned so much
While working with the full-grown beavers,
In helping them repair the dam,
And building it a little higher,
To deepen, widen out the pond,
Before the colder weather came.

Then suddenly young Tom awoke.
He rubbed his eyes; 'twas but a dream,
A dream, and yet so wonderful.
It changed his life in the years to be.
He said to himself, "This dream I'll live."
. . . .

And now he works in a lovely park.
He lives quite close to his friends, the beavers,
Happy to watch them in their ponds,
As they build their lodges and their dams,
And store up food for the winter months.

Ofttimes he whispers to himself,
"My boyhood dream, I live it now."

Fido, Our Cat, a Test of Faith

One morning as I rose from bed
And looked through window to the lawn,
Can you believe just what I saw?
'Twas Fido sitting happily perched
In the big tree where branches meet.

For we had sent Fido, our cat,
In box well closed, within a car,
To a new home we thought he'd like.
But now he sat where he used to sit
On one big crotch where the branches meet.

I'd heard and read of such strange things.
I doubted, wondered could they be.
But now I must recast my life,
Rebuild my faith through Fido's proof
That what I doubt I yet may see.

And so I sometimes feel there's born
Within the lives of cats and dogs,
Of birds, and ants, of fish, and bees
Some supra-sense, above, beyond
The senses that we use and know,
That acts as compass to their lives
To guide them on back home again.

One Day Our Skippy Came Not Home

One day our Skippy came not home.
He always knew the trail before.
But dogs at twelve are growing old.
The rhythm of their span of years,
It does not seem just one with ours.

I wonder if his sense of place
Was dimming now in Skippy's life.
Did he just lose the trail he knew,
He knew so well in days gone by?
Did he keep walking on and on
Till in some cool, sequestered nook
He lay upon the fresh, green grass,
And there he fell asleep and dreamed?

And in his dream did he find joy
In playing, romping on the lawn
With little kiddies whom he loved?
In begging titbits at the meal?
In following in his master's steps,
Amongst the trees, down by the lake,
Or lying near him on the green?

I cannot tell, but this I know
That our dog, Skippy, found a place
In memory's book within the home—
A place of joy for child and man.

Beyond Our Own

I sometimes feel there must be worlds
Far out in space beyond our own,
Where thinking beings like ourselves
Do live, and work, and ponder life.

Think you they're hoping to commune
With those who live in other spheres?
And will they in their reach of mind
Some day meet us, and we meet them?

If mind should learn to speak with mind
Would each have much of new to tell?
Would each rejoice to share the finest,
The loftiest thoughts his race had treasured?

'Tis just a fancy of my thinking,
But yet the fancies of the years
So oft have blossomed, borne rich harvest,
Been garnered by us as the real.

Saskatchewan, Saskatchewan

I once did see long years ago
An Indian chief, who, in his walk,
And in his fine, old wrinkled face
Showed pride of race, and justly so.
He stood nigh to the waters, swift,
That feed this river of the plains.
He seemed to stand on holy ground
As he raised his hand aloft and said,
"These mountains high, these woods, these streams,
They all were ours in days gone by."

This river flows past settlers' shacks,
Nigh quiet reserves where tepees stand.
This river flows through hamlets, small,
And busy cities of the plains.
This river is a symbol, real,
Of the moving tide of a virile race,
Of the onward march of pioneers,
Of their breadth of vision from these plains
That step by step through timeless years
Kept building, building prairie sod
By the lovely Kisiskatchewan.

"What's in a name?" the great bard asked.
I like the name passed on to us,
Passed on from the tongue of the native Crees.
I like the sound of this old name.
It sounds like the song of the flowing tide,
"Saskatchewan, Saskatchewan."

A Prairie Trail

This little story may I tell
This story of a prairie trail,
Just where it led, and what it meant
To two who knew and followed it?

You know those old, old trails, two ruts
Worn down by wheels of wagon loads,
And the tramp, tramp, tramp of horses' hoofs.
This trail, it curved between the bluffs,
And usually chose to round a hill.
Sometimes it just continued on
Right through the waters of a stream.
And yet it had one goal in view,
To tell to all, "Go west, go west."

An agent and an immigrant
Were driving o'er this winding trail.
The agent, he was selling land
To immigrants in quest of homes.
On either side there stretched for miles
The virgin, untouched prairie sod.

'Twas a lovely day on these great, broad plains.
A peace, a stillness filled the air,
Broken now, then once again
By the cheery song of a meadow lark.
And in the west, towards the setting sun,
Was a sky that lured them on and on
With its brilliant orange and yellow tints,
And little islets of fluffy clouds.

Dmitro touched the driver's hand.
They came to a halt on this prairie trail.
He pointed up to the sky beyond,
And in his broken English said,
"My Fader, your Fader; you and me, broders."

Throughout the years each bore in his heart
Rich memories of this prairie trail,
And this one thought yond all the others,
That each saw more than land, land, land,
For each saw God in sky and man.

I Like Your City, Saskatoon

A charming, prairie autumn day,
'Tis Indian summer, Nature's gift.
We just forget the cold and rain,
And breathe a silent prayer of thanks
For this brief season in between
When this year's warmth smiles its farewell.

On such a day within the park
A stranger stood and looked across
The waters of Saskatchewan,
And down along its winding course,
As north and east it wends its way.

The stranger stood and looked across
The waters of Saskatchewan.
His face, it told the joy he felt
To see the poplar and the birch,
That clothed the far bank of the stream,
All dressed in richest autumn garb
In blended reds, and browns, and yellows.

He paused beside me in the park,
Tall and neat in summer clothes,
With camera in its leathern case
To snap the loveliness he saw.
To me he made these traveller's comments,
"I travel west but once a year.
'Tis such a charming autumn day,
Along these banks, on down the stream.
I like your city, Saskatoon."

PART TWO

Fact and Fancy Interwoven

> Imagination bodies forth
> The forms of things unknown, the poet's pen
> Turns them to shapes, and gives to airy nothing
> A local habitation and a name.
> SHAKESPEARE, *A Midsummer Night's Dream.*

A Love That Fadeth Not Away

Two tots, a little girl, a little boy,
Before the years of school.
They lived the distance of four homes apart.
This was their world in which they lived and loved,
And there they found a kingdom all their own.

Sometimes they played at house.
The very stones were chairs and tables
That seemed to them so real.

They played at horse.
Two broomsticks were the horses.
At noontide hour they left their horses
In the shade along the kitchen wall.
They placed before them long, green grass to eat.

Often on a summer's day
They sat upon the step or on the green.
They talked and talked.
She lisped,
And often others knew not what she said.
But he knew.

Across the way, the old stone school.
The teacher watched them through the window of her room
She wondered what they talked about.
Their world of thought and fancy,
It was their very own.
. . . .
Years passed, and in her early teens
God called her to Himself.

Her friend of childhood
Knows not where she lives in God's Great Spirit World.
But this he knows
That in the eventide of his own life
Still she lives for him
A memory, sweet, of childhood love.

The world of childhood
Is so full of wonder, trust, and joy.
It adds a glory to the earth,
The glory of a love that's deep and pure,
A love that fadeth not away.

The Shepherd's Pipe

It's just a flute. This boy you see,
He made it from an old, old rifle,
That once belonged to some poor soul,
Who fought and died here in the valley.

This Arab boy, a shepherd lad,
He tends his sheep amongst the hills,
In the valleys nigh the Jordan,
The river Jordan, old in story.

He took the barrel from the rifle.
He filed it through to length that suited,
And from it fashioned what you see,
This flute, or shepherd's pipe you call it.

Through it his soul breathes melody.
Sometimes it is a plaintive air.
Sometimes it is so gay and mirthful.
In evening hours around the campfire
He plays old tunes for wandering tribesmen.

And now, just listen, he will play
A note of peace for you, a stranger,
To welcome you to come as guest
And share his master's humble living.
The stranger went and found rich welcome.
. . . .

And now years after midst world tensions,
Within himself this stranger wonders,
"Can we from this little story—
Rifle, boy, and shepherd's pipe—
Learn the secret of existence,
And live as neighbours to each other?"

Two young children playing with marbles
On the veldt lands, far down under.
Marbles, were they? Just some pebbles,
Little pebbles, round, and shiny.
They had found them in their rambles.

As they played they heard some footsteps,
Footsteps of a well built stranger.
Stranger paused, he looked, he marvelled:
"These are gems of rarest value."
Practised eyes discovered riches
In the marbles of these children.
He searched and searched; he found a fortune.

What do kiddies know of values,
Set by giants of trade and fashion,
In the world of grown-up mores?
For to them the so-called treasures
Were but playthings for their pleasures.

Do you ever sit and ponder
Little children's loves and interests,
Just how natural is their play life
In their world of fact and fancy,
Fact and fancy interwoven?

Can we carry with us, in us,
Something more of child-life splendour,
That will colour, tint our living
With a glory, bright and lasting?

Carpe Diem

"Carpe diem," wrote the poet
In the golden days of Rome.
Did he mean to seize the present,
Worry not about the morrow,
Live this day, enjoy its blessings,
Pluck it as a lovely flower
Midst the total of the days
That the fates assign to you?

"Carpe diem," quoth a card,
Christmas card a year ago
From a student far away.
Did he mean to tell to me
That in his school he meets each day,
Fills its hours with thoughtful study
That will feed our richest yearnings
With the best for Canada?

What Think You, Is There Merit in It?

I could repeat from memory
Both Iliad and Odyssey,
All that Homer wrote, bequeathed
Unto our race in poetry.

It was my father's way to teach
The lives of heroes of our people,
And slowly build within my mind
The sense, the feel of loveliness.

Thus wrote a Greek of long ago
Who served his race with sword and pen,
A man renowned throughout his land.
What think you, is there merit in it?

A Seeker after Truth

A seeker after truth was Alphonse.
In high esteem he held the Master—
A Frenchman, scholar, saint, and thinker—
"I wish so much I had your creed,
And then your life I'd gladly live it."

The Master paused, he thought a moment:
"Just live my life, my creed you'll find it."

The great man knew that words of creeds
Count not so much as some imagine.
Some creeds men learn, repeat by rote,
Though in their acts they rarely live them.
But let them heed the Master's vision,
Feel his touch, and living spirit,
Know his lead in loyal service,
Then they and he become one credo.

The Triumph of Her Spirit

This child, she could not use her arms
Like you or me to paint and draw,
So with a brush, held in her teeth,
She painted this, my Christmas card.

'Twas not the card, its picture, lettering,
It might have come from many others.
It was the heart that breathed the wish.
It was the will to try and try,
And if she failed, to keep on trying.
It was the thrill of joy and pride,
As her Christmas thought took form before her.
It was the triumph of her spirit.

Destined, Each for Other

Shah Jahan to Mumtaz Mahal,
"If the day should come that you must leave me,
A tomb I'll build like a lovely palace
In memory of my dearest Queen."

The Taj Mahal, it stands to-day,
Mausoleum, pure white marble,
Token of that promise given,
Joy, delight of all who view it.
Some say its beauty naught surpasses,
In all the world from east to west,
Loveliest architecture known.

But what is beauty wrought in marble
Compared with love that lives and speaks
From heart to heart in lives of two,
Who feel they're destined, each for other?

I Gazed into a Century

A hush fell o'er that little room,
As he repeated slowly, clearly
The psalmist's thoughts he learned in childhood:
"The Lord's my Shepherd, I'll not want."

I looked into his deep blue eyes.
I gazed into a century,
And in my heart I felt the thrill
Of a life I had not known before.

A debt we owe to those, our elders,
Who reach in age life's topmost years.
There must be something, strong, robust,
That rides the storms, the trials, the sorrows,
And gives their souls commanding height
To look back on the world they've travelled.

My friends, who still are young and strong,
Treat with respect those in the twilight.
You may not think they're wise as you,
But do you really understand them?
You have not lived the years of elders,
But they lived through the years of youth;
They know its passions, hopes, and challenge
Much better than you think they do.

My Work's My Prayer

On a tapestry, neatly woven,
In the entrance to a club-house
Standing mongst the spreading maples
On the bluffs above the lake shore
There I read a lovely credo,
Greeting thought of happy workers.
The opening words I still remember.
These they are, "My work's my prayer."

Years after in a teacher's classroom,
Neatly printed on a card
Standing forth where all might see them,
These words I read, "My work's my prayer."

'Twas the motto of this teacher
In her school upon the prairies,
Far away from craftsmen's club-house
On the heights above the lake shore.

Thoughts oft seem like fairy seedlings,
Carried far, no earth-born limits,
Taking root where they find welcome,
Growing, blooming, spreading fragrance.

PART THREE

I Travel at Leisure in the World of the Spirit

God is a Spirit: and they that worship Him
must worship Him in spirit and in truth.
ST. JOHN IV, 24.

Here in My Sanctum, My Cradle of Thinking

This suite where I live on this third upper storey
Is not large when compared with the homes of so many,
But in it and from it I travel and travel.

From my bed in the morning I look through the window
At the branches of trees as they bend in the breezes.
So graceful they seem with long arms reaching upwards.
In the cold winter months the trees and the birds
Are symbols that image the stream of the living,
And Nature's safe keeping of the life of her earth-world.

And here in my Sanctum, my Cradle of Thinking,
In this suite where I live on this third upper storey,
In fancy I roam with the poets and the prophets,
I share in the lives of great statesmen and masters,
Or in thought, silent thought, I commune with the Highest,
As I travel at leisure in the World of the Spirit.

That Day Stands Out Alone

So many days in life seem lost, forgotten.
That day stands out alone.

'Twas not the warmth and brightness of the summer's sun.
'Twas not the glad companionship of friends.
'Twas not the zest of life
In climbing upwards, upwards till our goal was reached.

It was a something more
Than human thought can fathom and can tell.
A something of the wonder that was ours.
The might and movement of the handicraft of time,
The sense of vastness,
Fold on fold, far as the human eye could reach.

Below us in the valley
A long thread wound in waves and curves,
The river that we knew so well,
Made small, so small in this its setting new,
Mongst lofty peaks, and cliffs, and headlands.
And here on this midsummer's day,
Covering the rugged northern slopes,
Were great, thick sheets of ice and snow,
As if the inmost life of summer
Had entered into compact with the winter snows,
A contract each felt bound to keep.

Over and above it all,
Man's soul was lifted
To the Soul that knows no bounds,
The Soul that is Infinite
In power, in majesty, in loveliness beyond compare.

I Wonder

If only I had eyes and the mind to interpret,
What wonders would I find in all Nature about me?
In the soil that I tread as I stroll through the valley?
The birds, as they gather the twigs and the grasses,
And fit them to the pattern of the life-world within them?
The bees, as they build up the combs with their honey?
The waters of the ocean, as they move up the beaches,
Or retreat with the tides far out o'er the shallows?
The sun, as it daily gives light to the earth-born?
The worlds without number in the far away spaces,
And the place they fulfil in the Scheme of Existence?

I wonder if the fish in the creek in the valley
Know aught of the lakes, of the seas, of the oceans,
In their vastness, their depths, their tides, and their motions.
Has the frog any memories of its days as a tadpole?
Has the dog, or the sheep, or the horse in my pasture
Any concept of prayer, any thought of the Godhead?
Do they ever build cairns, or altars, or temples
As symbols of mind in its reach towards the Infinite?

Yet down through the ages great seers and great prophets
Have fathomed the depths of the faith that's within them,
Of the meaning of life, of death, the hereafter,
Of the Real and the True beyond man's deepest vision,
That give end, and direction, and meaning, and purpose
To all that we see, that we love, that we hope for.

"What is man," asked the psalmist, "that of him Thou art mindful?
For him Thou hast crowned with glory and honour."

A World of Love and Mystery

Sometimes in thoughtful mood I lie
In sheltered clearance in the woods,
Or grassy knoll beside a stream,
Or rocky ledge whence I can gaze
At giant peaks midst slumbering clouds.
While in this mood I ofttimes feel
A kinship, bigger, richer far
Than any words that I can name,
With flowers, and birds, and trees, and hills,
With the One Power that moves through all
And makes this sense world that I see
A world of love and mystery.

The Immortal Bard

As I sit by my bookcase and roam through its volumes—
Windows to worlds I never can visit—
I share in the fancies and thoughts of the ages.
I ponder the meaning of the real world about me,
With its tensions, its doubts, its fears, its forebodings.
What future awaits if we see not our mission?

I pick up a volume of the great bard of England.
I wander o'er its pages. I pause. Will you listen?
  "Like the baseless fabric of this vision
  The cloud-capp'd towers, the gorgeous palaces,
  The solemn temples, the great globe itself,
  Yea, all which it inherit, shall dissolve,
  And, like this insubstantial pageant faded,
  Leave not a rack behind."
. . . .

Uncanny powers within himself
Prospero felt by fate belonged,
So long as staff and magic book
He kept to use as he might will,
To wreak destruction on his foes,
And vengeance take for all their wrongs.
A Spirit breathed the higher choice
To offer them forgiveness, love,
That they might all dwell in peace.
He listened to the Spirit's voice,
And his rough magic he abjured:
      "I'll break my staff,
  Bury it certain fathoms in the earth,
  And deeper than did ever plummet sound
  I'll drown my book."

Life's tempests, and life's passions stilled,
Mature in years, and in creative
Gifts through drama, sonnet, song,
Is this the bard, serene, and calm,
The Immortal Bard of Britain's isle,
Who speaks his last great thoughts unto
The world he loves?—Choose ye, not hate,
But choose forgiveness, peace, and love.

A blind poet fondly asked,
"Doth God exact day-labour, light denied?"
But in those sightless days,
To heights sublime his fancy soared
As his creative soul the answer found
While it pursued
"Things unattempted yet in prose or rhyme."

A searcher after truth,
Who lived his fourscore years
Within a few short miles of Königsberg, his boyhood home,—
His crippled, weakly frame
Imposed on him a constant, daily discipline in life,
But his rich mind found joy
In travelling deep and far within the Universe of Thought.

A master teacher,
Who left a lasting imprint on old England's Rugby School,—
When illness sapped his strength,
He thanked God for the pain.
The very suffering seemed a window
Through which there shone a light,
A light he had not truly felt before
Into the lives of struggling, sorrowing men.

A learnèd doctor,
Whom several lands were proud to call their own,—
On a little slip of paper
Were found these words,
Written in his closing hours of life,
"The Harbour almost reached after a splendid voyage
with such companions all the way and my boy awaiting me."*
So life, death, Life were merged in one.

*EDITH GITTINGS REID—*The Great Physician, Oxford University Press, p. 290.*

The Prophet,
Loveliest Son of Man,
The latchet of whose shoes, one said,
He was not worthy to unloose,—
The night before the Cross,
In the deep shadows of the Grove,
"O my Father,
If it be possible, let this cup pass from me:
Nevertheless not as I will, but as Thou wilt."

Some men there are,
Who through abiding faith,
And through their growing oneness with Eternal Mind
Transform the crosses of their lives
And in this triumph o'er the world
They find life's richest joy.

I Dreamed a Dream of the Realm of Being

I dreamed a dream of the Realm of Being,
Of the life in the beds of the ponds and the shallows,
The birds that sing to their mates at the dawning,
Little seeds that have fallen from blossoms above them,
Great trees that have grown from seedlings, so tiny,
The flowers in the meadows, the bees midst the nectar,
And all the wonders and beauties of Nature—
They sang in one chorus of the joy of Creation:
"Love is our Father, and loveliness our mission;
We live for our Father, we rejoice with the earth-born
That out of the Thought of Eternity's Being
We have grown and evolved these selves as you see them."

If We Keep Faith That It Is Real

If we keep faith that it is real,
As real and true for us to-day
As is the bread that we do eat,
As is the house in which we live,
This world will be a different place
From what it sometimes seems to be.

That it is real, the World Unseen,
Beyond the world of sense and touch.
That somewhere yond our farthest ken,
And yet within our deepest self,
There is the Self that's more than we,
The First Cause, Mind-Force, Power Supreme,
Who endless through his Timeless Time
Creates, and fashions, works, and builds.
That He projects Himself through space
In countless worlds we little know,
In countless more we just surmise.

If we keep faith that this is true,
As true and real for us to-day
As is the bread that we do eat,
As is the house in which we live,
This world will be a different place
From what it sometimes seems to be.

Life's Orbit

Not long ago I searched the sky
As daylight fell and stars peeped forth,
When lo! I saw or thought I saw
The comet that the learnèd found
Far out in space. They tell us that
It pays to us one visit brief
And then 'tis gone to travel far,
Far on through Nature's vast unknown.

Sometimes I see this self of mine,
This little self, all busied with
The thoughts, and cares, and daily round
Of duties here on earth. And yet
Some say man's true abiding self
Is a spark from out the Eternal Mind,
The Mind that calls us to Himself,
And if we answer to the call
We find the orbit of our lives
Linked with the Universe of God.

The Quest of Marsyas

NOTE BY THE AUTHOR—The Quest of Marsyas symbolizes the longing of a learned Greek to know something of the person and the teaching of Jesus. Marsyas is represented as making his home thirty miles east of the Jordan in Gerasa, one of the cities of the Decapolis, and a noted centre of Graeco-Roman culture. The remains of Gerasa with its temple to Artemis, theatre, forum, circus, fountains, baths have been described by various travellers to the Holy Land, including Morton in his book, "In the Steps of the Master."

The poem puts into the mouth of Mary of Bethany the joy of her life in her meeting with Jesus, as told in St. Luke's Gospel, chapter x, 38-42.

Oh, Marsyas, you ask me to tell about Jesus,
As here in this garden He spoke of his mission.
Will a Greek of the schools of Athens and Ephesus
List to a woman of the village of Bethany
As she pictures the Master to one who's not known Him?

One day in this garden I shall always remember.
I sat at his feet in this garden of Bethany,
I sat at his feet all lost in his teaching.
He told me of the love of our Father in Heaven.
It shone in the face of the Christ in the garden.
It reached to the fallen with the voice of a Saviour,
Touched the life of the mourner, breathing hope in man's sorrows.
It spoke to the hungry of a Bread that's Eternal,
And called men to worship in the Kingdom of Heaven.

"The one thing that is needful," I, Mary, had chosen:
These were the words of Jesus, the Master.
This one thing has been mine from that day till the present,
Since I felt in this Rabbi, this Guest in our garden,
The life of the Spirit of the God of our fathers.
It lifted me upwards to the Soul of Creation,
It filled my whole self with a joy beyond telling.

In the cool of the evening, down the pathway from Bethany
Slowly walked Marsyas towards the join with the highway.
Sometimes he paused, breathed the beauty of sunset.
For the beauty of meadows, of trees, and of mountains,
Of sunsets, of children, of fancies of poets,
Of thoughts of the schoolmen, of maidens, of mothers,
In the soul of this Greek, they all had a lodging,
A heritage rich from the Gods of his fathers.

On the slope of Mount Olivet, as it looks towards the City,
He rested, and pondered the story of Mary.

His mind wandered back o'er the days of his childhood
To his home in Gerasa, on the banks of the Jabbok.
As a boy he found joy in the Gods of his fathers,
As a student delved deeply into the temple of learning.
He lived in the realm of Ideas, Ideals,
As he searched for life's meaning, the First Cause, the Final.
But something seemed lacking in his pattern of thinking.
"The one thing that is needful," to-day have I found it
In the joy of this Woman through her faith in the Master?
Is this Rabbi from Nazareth in his person, his teaching,
God's answer to man, as the Son of the Highest,
Living Word of the Father?—I shall search till I find Him.
. . . .

Marsyas searched. He found the Master,
And through the Master found himself.

Mnemosyne, Memory Fond

Mnemosyne, Memory fond, some said
Thou wert a Goddess fair, and the Muses children
Of thy love. Whoe'er thou art, one thing
I know that thou and thine were with me here
To-night. For as I sat alone, or seeming
So, I listened to sweet music o'er
The air. Visions, too, of the yesteryears
Flashed o'er my mind. So many happy scenes
Seemed just to knock, pay greeting, then were gone.
But a lonely night was changed, transformed into
A night of cheer. Farewell for now. May I
Again, and often once again, with thee
And with the Muses live and love. And to
The Power Supreme I offer thanks that thou
Hast not forgot me in these later years.

I Trust Somehow I Share Your Joy

My readers, if you now have read
Between the covers of this book,
And found some thoughts that to you speak
And bring to you an inner joy,
Then, though I may be distant far,
I trust somehow I share your joy.